REVELATIONS UNSEALED:

WHEN A COINCIDENCE COINCIDES

BY EMMANUEL SOLOMON

THE WORLD
IS IN YOUR HANDS LLC

REVELATIONS UNSEALED: When a coincidence coincides

TO: ESTELLA "LADY" JONES,

the virgin who gave birth.

REVELATIONS UNSEALED: When a coincidence coincides

REVELATIONS UNSEALED: When a coincidence coincides

"I will change the way that man sees the world."

Minister Emmanuel Solomon

For it is by my very design they will call me a conman and say that I am a confederacy.
"Say ye not, A confederacy, to all them to whom this people shall say, A confederacy; neither
fear ye their fear, nor be afraid." (*Isaiah* 8:12)

REVELATIONS UNSEALED: When a coincidence coincides

INTRODUCTION

I will use the word God, Most High God, and ANU interchangeably, for they are the same.

There are two different species in this world. These species are controlled by brothers named Enki and Enlil. These brothers have been engaging in an age-long war for dominion of this world. Their father ANU, is on his way to resolve this conflict by destroying this world and starting a new world.

Next to God alone, *blood* is used more than any other word in the bible. This is of huge importance! Enki & Enlil dominion is separated only by blood. My mother's blood type is O negative, no A or B particles, no rhesus particles; therefore her blood is considered pure, like a virgin. I am O positive. My birth represents a paradigm shift. For you CANNOT just become king; it has always been about bloodline! That is why all the Royal Family and US Presidents are of RH negative decent, they are an advanced species. This is by the design of Enlil.

Nature is divided into four categories.

Examples:

Spring	Summer	Fall	Winter
Earth	Water	Air	Fire
North	South	East	West
Man	Woman	Boy	Girl

Numerology is a buzzword for sacred geometry. Everything in this universe is calculated; nothing is by chance. God's holy number is seven. Once the number seven is placed in all four categories (soul, destiny, life path, simple gematria) on a birth chart, a prophet is present.

Example:

Soul	Destiny	Life Path	Simple Gematria
7	**7**	**7**	**7**

REVELATIONS UNSEALED: When a coincidence coincides

No man breathing is worthy of praise or glory, that belongs to The Most High God alone. Unlike myself, God was never subject to breath! I claim the personification of ANU, the messenger, the great prophet.

In 2019 to test my strength, ANU allowed me to undergo a humiliation ritual. I cannot stress it enough that opposition is necessary. Mentally all warriors, just like precious stones, must be broken down and then refined (**READ** *Zechariah* 13:9). In other words, only under extreme stress can DNA be unlocked. Without this epigenetic effect, this book would not be possible. Because of my refinement in 2019, I see life differently, literally.

My mission is to WAKE UP THE SLEEPING GIANT! I wish to deliver peace by restoring order. I am here to resurrect the ancient science of spirituality, better known as serpent knowledge. I am here to prepare my kind for ANU's return and warn others of his wrath. For thunder & lightning spoke to me by saying, "The World Is In Your Hands."

According to today's media, a freedom fighter is equivalent to being a domestic terrorist. Debauchery is embraced, while morals are viewed with disdain. No longer can they force their lifestyle on us. Judgment is on the way; I pray that you are on the right side, beloved.

For nearly two thousand years, the book of Revelations has remained a mystery. The reason for this mystery is simple, they did not want you to know the truth. Oh, how much more I would have liked to remain anonymous. I take no pleasure by being so intimate with the world; however, this is what The Most High God requires of me. In the age that we are entering, secrets no longer exist.

REVELATIONS UNSEALED: When a coincidence coincides

CHAPTER 1

DECODING THE WORLD

I implore you to carefully consider every word of this letter as if your life depended on it, for it very may will. Your bloodline or blood type is determined by antigens being either present or absent. Antigens are 1st classified by the RH factor, then they are grouped into the categories of: O, A, B, or AB.

Now hold on tight…this is where the ride begins.

Antigen is a compound word. It consists of the word ANTI + GENE = ANTIGEN. The word 'anti' derives from the word 'Antaeus'. According to the Berbers & Greeks, Antaeus was a giant that lived in Morocco. Now, look at the word again.

A N T I G E N
                    I
                    A
                    N
                    T

ANTIGEN IS HOW THEY TRACK THE GIANT GENE!!!

BLOOD TYPES

O   A   B   AB

Original Blood   Aboriginal Blood

REVELATIONS UNSEALED: When a coincidence coincides

Yesterday's strife and discord are gone in the wind.

For today marks a new beginning.

By now, one might wonder what my credentials are? Or better yet, whom am I? Fret not, I will tell you both. On multiple occasions, my father told me that during a dream, God instructed him on what to name me. A good name is rather to be chosen than great riches (*Proverbs* 22:1).

SOLOMON   EMMANUEL   JONES

1 / 10 / 1985

SOUL	7		
DESTINY	7	■ FOUR	7'S
LIFE PATH	7		
SIMPLE GEMATRIA	7		

I am called by name only twice in the Old Testament. Pay close attention to what scriptures say my name.

Isaiah 7: 14   &   Isaiah 8: 8   =   16

7 7 7   ✚   7

■ FOUR 7'S

REVELATIONS UNSEALED: When a coincidence coincides

The mathematicians, secret keepers, and those in high places know the truth, isn't it time you do too? Anytime God's holy number 7 is placed in all four categories of a birth chart, a prophet is present.`

Picture from *BRUCE ALMIGHTY*

Who else can gather the scattered from the four corners of the world?

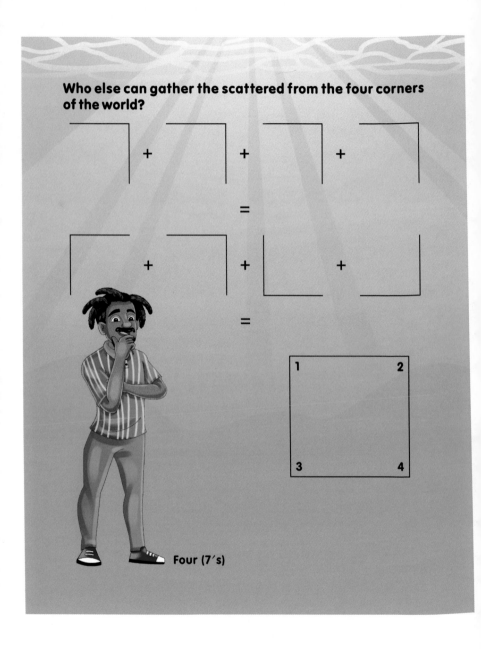

Four (7's)

Whom else can restore perfect harmony with the most high God?

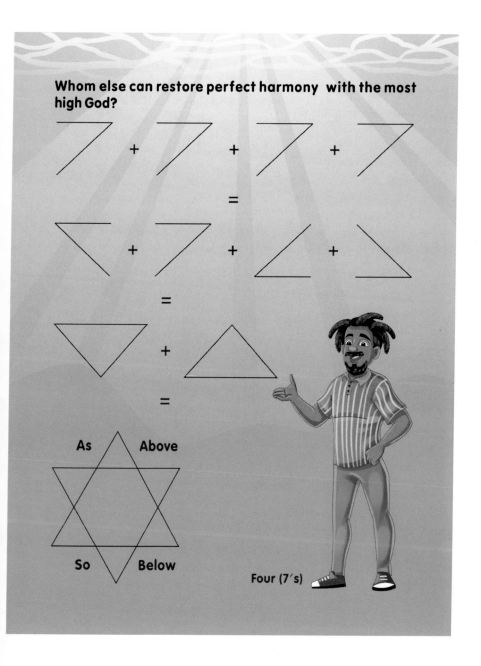

As Above

So Below

Four (7's)

REVELATIONS UNSEALED: When a coincidence coincides

REVELATIONS UNSEALED: When a coincidence coincides

Every knee shall bow!

Four (7′s)

REVELATIONS UNSEALED: When a coincidence coincides

'Therefore the Lord himself shall give you a sign; Behold a virgin shall conceive and bear a son, and shall call his name Imanuel.' *Isaiah 7:14.*

The mathematicians, secret keepers, and those in high places know the truth, isn't it time you do too? Imanuel is coded, (im-ANU-el) = **3 Names of God**. When it comes to this type of word magic, vowels can be omitted and are interchangeable; consonants that are repeated tend to be reduced to only one.

EXAMPLE: **Emmanuel = Emanuel = Immanuel = Imanuel**

Now pay close attention to the 'virgin birth' in the above scripture. I will tell you how I fit the mold. According to western astrology, my mother, who is a Virgo born August 30, 1957, gave birth to me on a Virgo moon. Now although virgin is synonymous with Virgo, it is superseded by another word. Virgin equates to pure bloods (RH negative). Study kingship, RH negative blood has long been considered pure/virgin blood, because it is not tainted with animal blood. All the Royal families and the majority of US Presidents have been stated to belong to RH negative bloodline (virgin blood).

Like any worthy messiah, my birth represents a paradigm shift. Upon my arrival, the purebloods will no longer rule. This is important to comprehend! Suspension of hostilities between the bloodlines would not be a possibility if ANU did not design it as such. For crying out loud, what God-fearing man would curse the bloodline that gave him birth?

The only type of being (animal or human) capable of a virgin birth is the NAGA. NAGA means serpent. The serpent, throughout the ages, has been depicted eating its own tail. Us as the serpent people, this symbolizes our immortality; we have no beginning and no end.

D E C O D I N G   ISAIAH CHAPTER 7:14

Therefore the Lord himself (ANU) shall give you a sign; Behold a pure-blooded, O negative NAGA, shall conceive and bear a son, and shall call his name IM-ANU-EL.

'Butter and Honey shall he eat that he may know to refuse the evil and choose the good. For before the child shall know to refuse the evil and choose the good, the land that thou abhorrest shall be forsaken of both her kings.' *Isaiah 7:15-16*

D E C O D I N G   ISAIAH CHAPTER 7:15-16

Just like the most high most God, Imanuel has known both good and evil (see Isaiah 45:7). To be all-knowing, you must know both good and evil. Imanuel shift of consciousness was a result of a dietary change.

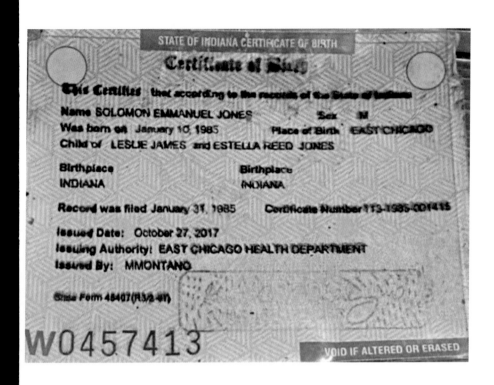

State Form 48407(R3/2-17)

W0457413

VOID IF ALTERED OR ERASED

SOLOMON   EMMANUEL   JONES

1 / 10 / 1985

SOUL	7		
DESTINY	7	■ FOUR	7'S
LIFE PATH	7		
SIMPLE GEMATRIA	7		

REVELATIONS UNSEALED: When a coincidence coincides

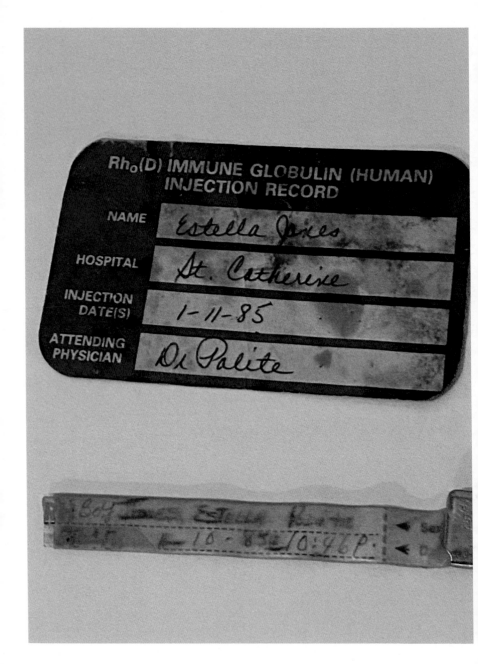

REVELATIONS UNSEALED: When a coincidence coincides

I WILL DECODE WHAT HAS BEEN HIDDEN IN REVELATIONS

13 And when the dragon saw that he was cast unto the earth, he persecuted the woman which brought forth the man child.

14 And to the woman were given two wings of a great eagle, that she might fly into the wilderness, into her place, where she is nourished for a time, and times, and half a time, from the face of the serpent.

15 And the serpent cast out of his mouth water as a flood after the woman, that he might cause her to be carried away of the flood.

16 And the earth helped the woman, and the earth opened her mouth, and swallowed up the flood which the dragon cast out of his mouth.   *Revelations 12:13-16*

How many times have you asked your pastor for clarity on the book of Revelations? Never once have you received a clear answer! Either they emit some foolish analogy or worst, they settle you in ignorance by saying, "God doesn't want us to know at this time."

I have the zeal of ANU! I can explain what your pastors simply cannot. Not only will I break down the above scripture, but I will show you NAGAS why we are the serpent people literally. I will show you why our land Amaruca a.k.a. America, is called Turtle Island. I will show you the serpent who beguiled Eve; hence only the Naga and European have RH negative blood. But first, I have a question, why do you let them teach you how to see?

NAGA now is the time to see like a GOD!

ROTATE

YOUR

MAP

REVELATIONS UNSEALED: When a coincidence coincides

And when the dragon saw that he was cast unto the earth, he persecuted the woman which brought forth the man child

COINCIDENCE OR DOES THIS COINCIDES WITH THE TRUTH?

REVELATIONS UNSEALED: When a coincidence coincides

And the earth helped the woman, and the earth opened her mouth, and swallowed up the flood which the dragon cast out of his mouth.

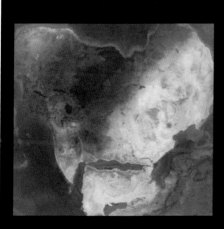

COINCIDENCE OR DOES THIS COINCIDES WITH THE TRUTH?

REVELATIONS UNSEALED: When a coincidence coincides

COINCIDENCE OR DOES THIS COINCIDES WITH THE TRUTH?

- [13] And when the dragon saw that he was cast unto the earth, he persecuted the woman which brought forth the man child.

- [14] And to the woman were given two wings of a great eagle, that she might fly into the wilderness, into her place, where she is nourished for a time, and times, and half a time, from the face of the serpent.

- [15] And the serpent cast out of his mouth water as a flood after the woman, that he might cause her to be carried away of the flood.

- [16] And the earth helped the woman, and the earth opened her mouth, and swallowed up the flood which the dragon cast out of his mouth. *Rev 12:13-16*

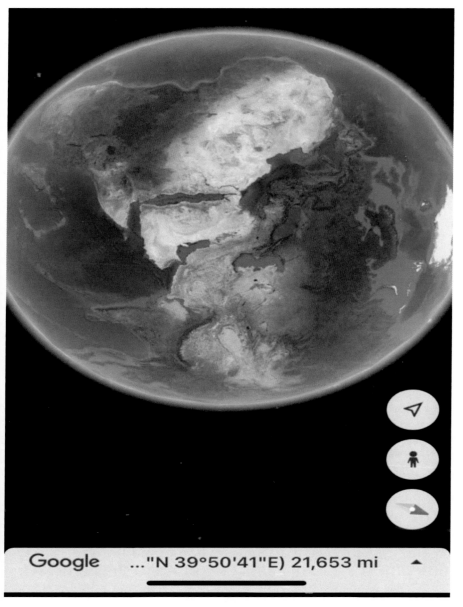

Google   ..."N 39°50'41"E) 21,653 mi   ▲

COINCIDENCE OR DOES THIS COINCIDES WITH THE TRUTH?

REVELATIONS UNSEALED: When a coincidence coincides

This is why Turtle island Is home of The Serpent

Here is the Serpent who Beguiled Eve

COINCIDENCE OR DOES THIS COINCIDES WITH THE TRUTH?

REVELATIONS UNSEALED: When a coincidence coincides

Naga Nose

LET US MAKE MAN IN OUR IMAGE

One of the biggest drawbacks of living in this gumbo pot we call America, is the fact we quite often confuse racial pride with racial hatred. Let me make this clear, just because I have a sense of pride DOES NOT equate me to a race warrior. Does the economist get labeled *racist*, by reporting the fact black people's resoucres are in an inferior position? No! Then neither should I, simple because I tell an uncomfortable truth. While speaking of economics, can you imagine the psychological damage it renders NAGA parents each time they give their children a dollar?

REVELATIONS UNSEALED: When a coincidence coincides

CHAPTER 2

UNSEALING TRUTHS

Woe to the astrologers who put price tags on reading God's lights! You are no better than the damned! In our land Turtle Island, we were religiously in tune with nature and the cosmos; Christianity, Islam, Judaism, and Buddhism all originated from the dragon's land. All religion bears the mark of the beast.

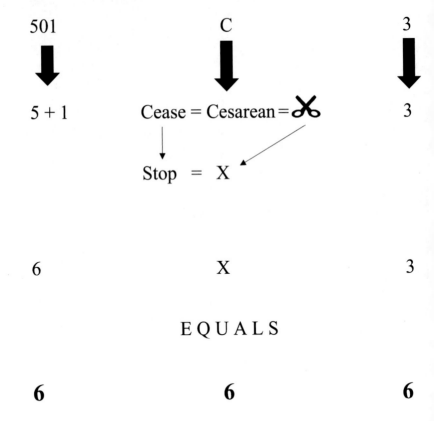

REVELATIONS UNSEALED: When a coincidence coincides

Obesity, aids, cancer, herpes, sickle cell, asthma, kidney & liver disease are all incurable, according to western science; it is evident that doctors do not have all the answers. Criminal injustice has run rampant in our land; lawmakers do not have all the answers. Serpent knowledge, aka NAGA knowledge, derives from our land. All formal education derives from the dragon's land, not ours. The Rockefeller family are RH Negative.

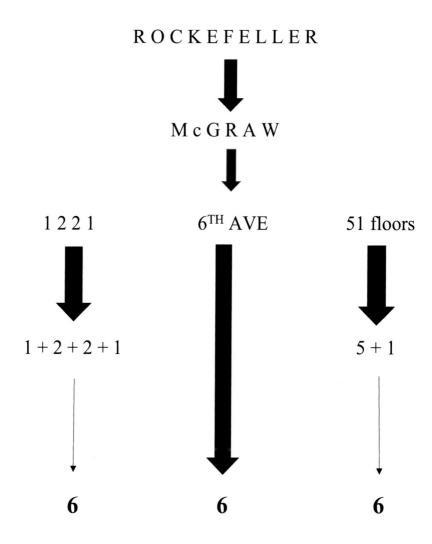

ROCKEFELLER

McGRAW

1 2 2 1   6TH AVE   51 floors

1 + 2 + 2 + 1   5 + 1

6   6   6

REVELATIONS UNSEALED: When a coincidence coincides

On July 4 of 1776, three men whose ancestors originate from the dragon's crown came together and developed this Great Seal. Within twenty-five years, two of the three men became president. Now pay close attention because here comes the kicker; exactly fifty years later, those presidents died on the same day, July 4 of 1826. Seal means to fasten or close securely; so what is inside this Great Seal? The mathematicians, secret keepers, and those in high places know, isn't time that you do too?

GREAT   SEAL

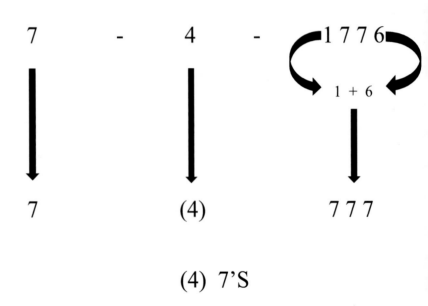

(4) 7'S

*Remember the significance of (4) 7's. Now since we have busted open this "Great Seal," let us see what is inside. To look at this in-depth, you will need a one-dollar bill. On the back of the note, we see "Annuit Coeptis." Annuit Coeptis means God has favored our undertakings (yes, your government knows ANU means God). Followed by the Roman numerals MDCCLXXVI, which equals 1776, referring to the year the seal was signed. Lastly, we see "Novus Ordo Seclorum," which is Latin for New Age World.

Let us rejoice the seal has been broken! ANU (7777) has delivered us back to the glory days of Saturn, which is better known as the Age of Aquarius.

REVELATIONS UNSEALED: When a coincidence coincides

The Aquarian Age is the age of knowing.

- Know that Albion was the home of the albino. Albion is now called England.

- Know that pharaohs were ferals.

- Know that name and story of Mosses & Rames mirrors Romulus & Remus!

- Know why they said, 'thou shall not kill" instead of "thou shall not murder."
  Kill = /Kəl/ = Cull. Cull is selective breeding based on desired characteristics.

- Know that "rod" means scion. Scion is used for grafting.

- Know that we NAGAs are the copper-colored natives of this earth.

- Know that a cop's original name was copper.

- Know that the forerunner /ˈfôrˌrənər/ has become the foreigner.

- Know that their Lord instructed them to celebrate a Passover fearing my return, on the 1st-month 10th day (Exodus 12:2-3)

- Know the energy of that date 1st-month 10th day, for did they not fear Rasputin?

- Know that they cannot govern a supreme body; this violates universal law!

- Know that fear is a useless emotion; everything is written. Fate over faith!

Know that metal is for the mental. Remove the dross from the silver and drink! By consuming large quantities of nanoparticles of silver, I have seen the tree of knowledge of good and evil. This tree is guarded by serpents. America, Amaruca, Turtle Island, or whatever else you choose to call it, this is serpent's land. Naga, nigga, nigger, or whatever you want to call us, we are the serpent people.

Divine intervention is on the way; be ready and steadfast. ANU will be conducting a DNA test, and animal consumption not only taints your blood, but it also lowers your vibration. My primary reason for veganism is not an ethical one, but more so spiritual-based. My visions and overall intuition have skyrocketed since converting to a plant-based diet nine years ago.

REVELATIONS UNSEALED: When a coincidence coincides

CHAPTER 3

THIS IS A WATER WORLD

Once Nagas grasp the relationship between water and copper, then they value themselves as God's chosen people. Our land Turtle Island contains the majority of the world's freshwater! The most valuable natural resource on earth lives here in Amaruca.

But if a woman have long hair, it is a glory to her: for her hair is given for a covering.

1 Corinthians 11:15

The mathematicians, secret keepers, and those in high places know the truth, isn't it time you do too? Covering is a compound word. Cove + ring = Covering. Cove is a ***Hebrew word*** defining a circular or round entrance always connected with water. Only Nagas hair contain a covering.

REVELATIONS UNSEALED: When a coincidence coincides

ONLY THE NAGA HAIR HAS A COVE-RING

REVELATIONS UNSEALED: When a coincidence coincides

REVELATIONS UNSEALED: When a coincidence coincides

Let them lie to you no longer; the moon is a magnet. Why does the moon control the tides of the ocean and not the lakes? It is because the oceans are filled with minerals/metals. For eons, women have been linked to the moon, which was initially named sin; however after colonialization, the word sin was made synonymous with evil. Women are governed by the moon; the moon is a magnet; therefore, we deem women attractive. Be careful about whom you find attractive; plenty of women have guided good men to prison or an early grave.

Admittedly by being magnetically pulled to women that I found attractive ultimately guided me like a compass to discovering a great deal of what I know today. It was Sista Shannon that lead me to veganism nine years ago. Mayah was the one who introduced me to sidereal astrology, the best composition of the night sky. Vera decoded my name 1st, for Imanuel equals Im ANU el, the three names of God! Sexual attraction does not equate to sexual activity; I touched none of these women.

Another example of how female attraction indirectly led me to knowledge. My child's mother, Kayla, was pressured to take a RhoGAM shot during her doctor visit. The doctor told her that since she has O negative blood, this injection would safeguard our baby from deadly antibodies. HUH? Being a holistic man and desiring a natural pregnancy, this did not sit well with me. Immediately I immersed myself into research on exactly what this shot was all about. A couple thousand hours after investigating this matter, all the while conducting blood type tests for my whole family, a divine download, and to my surprise, my mother was given the same injection to ensure my survival.

Another example of how female attraction indirectly led me to knowledge. My ex-wife comes from a small-town call Paducah, Kentucky. I never heard of Paducah prior to meeting her at the age of twenty-five. Recently I discovered that Paducah produced and held this country's uranium. Uranium equals nuclear power! This is a fact that she is still unaware of to this day.

Lastly, another female I was attracted to help me to learn telepathy. By her deep gazes accompanied only with silence, I learned the power of the unspoken language. Honesty is key, for the eyes never lie. It is a necessity that we pay close attention to the eyes; facial masks are for real; they have perfected this practice.

Not one of these women lead me directly, no that's masculine; and I follow no woman nor man. It was subtle energy like the moon that help point me in the right direction. It was so indirect that without analyzing the situation, one might not even notice.

REVELATIONS UNSEALED: When a coincidence coincides

I HAVE FULL SUPPORT OF THE WATER

7 ✖ (4)

DAYS   WEEKS

=

MOON CYCLE

FOUR (7's)

There are twenty-eight days in a *moon cycle* and thirteen *moon cycles* in a year. Nature testifies my legitimacy! Have you not examined a turtle's shell? Multiply the 28 outer rings of any turtle times the 13 inner rings, and there is your calendar. It can be several books written on why they canceled the number 13 from society.

CHAPTER 4

THE FATHER (ANU), SON (ENKI), & HOLY SPIRIT (ENLIL)

Cain & Abel

Jacob & Esua

Issac & Ishmel

Joseph & brothers

All these stories share the same theme; the younger brother receives the blessing. Anunnaki's story is no different. ANU's firstborn son Enki was sent to rule over the earth. Later Anu's second-born son Enlil came to earth and claimed rulership. Ever since Enlil's arrival, they have been at odds over rightful kingship. ANU loves both of his sons; so settle this dispute, ANU is on his way back to destroy this world with fire and start a new world.

EN – LORD

KI – EARTH   ENKI – LORD OF THE EARTH

LIL – AIR   ENLIL – LORD OF THE AIR

Although both are ANU's sons and they both came from the heavens, Enki & Enlil (nowadays called named Satan and Lucifer) do not share the same identity. Satan, aka Enki, is the prince of inner earth, while Lucifer aka Enlil, is the prince of the air.

EPHESIANS $2:2$ JOB

"The morning star", "The fallen star", "The holy spirit", "The God of breath,", Lucifer aka Enlil, has many titles. The morning star was also called Venus; at one point, Venus was called Isis. The genealogical lineage or simply put "Genes" of Isis is where we get the name Genesis. If money is

REVELATIONS UNSEALED: When a coincidence coincides

the root of all evil…. Then what day is payday? Friday and Friday belong to Venus! So the next time you hear someone say, "Thank God it's Friday," just know that the God they are referring to is Enlil, aka Lucifer.

There are two different species of people on this earth. The 1st species was created by Enki in Genesis 1:26; the 2nd species was formed by Enlil, God of Breath, in Genesis 2:7. Read Genesis 3:15, does it not fit the mold of pregnancy of an RH negative woman impregnated by an RH positive man? Separated by blood, they cannot reproduce WITHOUT medical intervention. Examine their blood flow. Can this be why they say water and oil do not mix? Throughout the ages, Enlil, aka Lucifer, God of the Air, has been symbolized as a bird. The man that Enlil controls was formed from breath in Genesis chapter 2 has been depicted as half man/half bird.

EXAMPLES OF LUCIFERIAN TRADEMARK

- Larry Bird
- Venus Williams
- 2pac = Birdie
- Michael "AIR" Jordan
- Byrdgang aka Dipset
- Bird = kilo of cocaine
- Sue Bird
- Birdman and Lil Wayne

Now see why there are so many *superstar* planes crashing. It symbolizes Lucifer, the bright morning *star* fall from heaven; think about it. Now see the ritual you are engaging in; by committing 8hrs (that is 1/3 of your compacity) into a fallen state, didn't Lucifer accompanied with a third of the angels enter a fallen state? Now see why the only unforgivable sin is blasphemy against the Holy Spirit, not against The Most High God but the Holy Spirit.

Lucifer, the God of the Air, wants us, the serpent people, to *get high*. Do not continue falling for this trap; we must stay vigilant. Knowledge does not dwell in chaos; drugs are a repellant to The Most High God. Naga, you are the serpent they cursed! Adder is the name of a serpent; now see how Adderall was designed to harm all of you, Naga! The serpent was the father/**Co**-parent of **Cain** (Genesis 4:1); now see how **cocaine** is a drug designed to harm you, Naga! The serpent was cursed to eat dust (Genesis 3:14); now see how Angel-dust is dust for the Angels, aka the sons of God, that is us, Naga! Fear not their time is dwindling; that is the real reason why we hear the slogan "I can't Breathe."

REVELATIONS UNSEALED: When a coincidence coincides

SATURN

VENUS

Notice the Cove-Rings of Saturn!

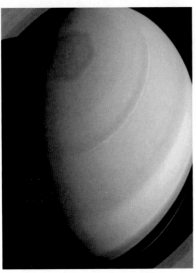

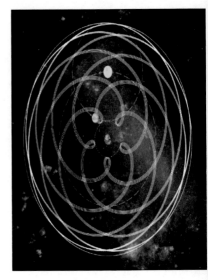

6 POINT STAR

5 POINT STAR

If there is not an actual pentagram or hexagram in the heavens, why do we draw stars as such?

- Every eight years, Venus makes a perfect pentagram around the constellations.

- On Saturn's north pole seats a hexagram.

Polydactyly is a condition when a person is born with six fingers or six toes. Roughly 1 out of 100 Nagas in Amaruca are born with a sixth finger or toe; this is the way my son was born. Having a 6th digit is a trait of the Giants (2 Samuel 21:20). My mission is to **WAKE UP THE SLEEPING GIANT!** In 2002, there were only eight newborns with polydactyly reported in the UK. Yet we are all the same? Before we were converted to the base 10 counting system, we used the based 12 counting. We made that system using our digits. Jewelers know why 12 ounces are in a pound, just like mason knows why 12 inches are in a foot. Nowadays, racial attacks are covert, so you must pay attention. Sars is the unit of time the Anunnaki used to measured; coincidentally, it is the official name of Covid 19.

REVELATIONS UNSEALED: When a coincidence coincides

Solomon Emmanuel Jones JR.

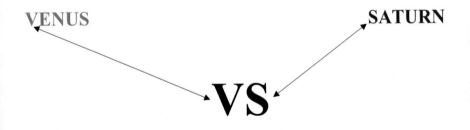

VENUS   SATURN

VS

ALSO CALLED

Lucifer	Satan
Enlil	Enki
Dragon	Serpent
Vain/Vanity	Knowledge
God of Air/Breath Earth	God of

Now see why the God of Breath opposed *mankind* from having knowledge. Now see why the most knowledgeable ever, King Solomon hated vanity. Now see why the serpent and the dragon battle in Revelations. What separates earthlings from the heavens if it is not the air? Maybe that is why some religions preach that you cannot have a direct relationship with The Most High God. They say that you must deliver your message to a lesser God, that will eventually relay your message.

Consider how the different creation stories in Genesis chapter 1&2, perfectly parallel with the parable of wheat and tares located in Matthew 13:24-30.

1. God created everything *good.*   The farmer created everything *good.*
2. God *rested.*   The farmer *rested.*
3. *Lord God* formed man out of dust.   His *Enemy* came and sowed tares.

The parable did not lie, aboriginal bloodlines (A, B, and AB) are an abomination aka the tares and they will burnout literally; the original man (O blood) aka the wheat will be gathered to safety. I have seen this vision.

REVELATIONS UNSEALED: When a coincidence coincides

CHAPTER 5

AMBASSADOR OF PEACE

My message to the RH Negatives:

I am not here for anything other than peace! And trust me, bloodshed is the last thing that you would ever want. Did I not come thru the portal of an RH negative woman whom I love dearly? Does 7 not equate to peace? For my very birth is a testament to my sincerity. I value kingship because it was sent from the heavens. I grasp why people were kept in the dark, however, that time has ended. No longer will you lead the masses.

My message to the RH Positives:

Repent Serpent! Peace means the very opposite of piece; peace means wholeness. Harmony and tranquility are a result of peace, not the definition. When we all come together, we will get wholeness, we will get peace!

Repent Serpent! For the time is near and the truth is stranger than fiction. Your copper-colored carbon body is a spacesuit; your hair's cove-ring is a vortex. The mothership that the ancients spoke about is real. This world will burn, and only The Most High God chosen people will be saved. Some might feel more comfortable calling this event the 'Rapture'.

Repent Serpent! Turn away from your wicked ways or perish. All evil is equal. Abortion is no holier than murder; a life is a life. Lying is no holier than stealing; both are deceitful. Lesbianism is no holier than homosexuality; neither brings forth fruit. Adultery is no holier than rape, your body is one with your partner, and they did not consent for it to be given away.

Repent Serpent! Naga, we have been given two simple laws: Be fruitful and multiply & let fruit-bearing seed be your meat.

Repent Serpent! Know that our family, the very ones that must be saved, is the so-called:

- Coon & Sellout
- Finessers & Charmers
- Gays & Lesbians
- Whores & Whoremongers
- Dope fiends
- Thugs

Repent Serpent! Be not ashamed; we all fell short of the glory of God. It takes strength to overcome these types of spirits we are battling. I am only interested in seeing the good in you Naga, for I am the prince of peace.

REVELATIONS UNSEALED: When a coincidence coincides

CHAPTER 6

INSIDE LOOK

Out of kindness I share my message. I pride myself on my sobriety. I am a full-time father to my five beautiful children. I have no personal social media accounts to request you follow me on. I am fully aware of the enemies my truth will create. So with all this considered, ask yourself why, why would a sane individual draft such a message? The answer is simple, I have been possessed by the zeal of The Most High God. Come let me share with you, my chart; it will testify my story. You cannot fake the position I claim; the stars do not lie.

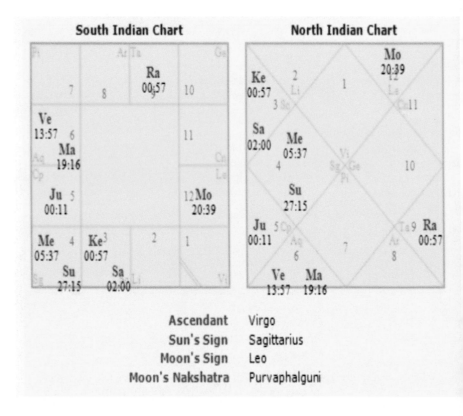

REVELATIONS UNSEALED: When a coincidence coincides

Planetary Details

	Deg	Sign	Nakshatra	Pada	Ld/SL
Asc	10:02	Virgo	Hasta	1	Mo / Mo
Sun	27:15	Sagittarius	Uttarashadha	1	Su / Su
Moon	20:39	Leo	Purvaphalguni	3	Ve / Ju
Mars	19:16	Aquarius	Satabhisha	4	Ra / Ma
Mercury	05:37	Sagittarius	Mula	2	Ke / Ra
Jupiter	00:11	Capricorn	Uttarashadha	2	Su / Ra
Venus	13:57	Aquarius	Satabhisha	3	Ra / Me
Saturn	02:00	Scorpio	Visakha	4	Ju / Ra
Rahu	00:57	Taurus	Krittika	2	Su / Ra
Ketu	00:57	Scorpio	Visakha	4	Ju / Ma

- Out of kindness I share my message – Purva Phalguni.
- I pride myself on my sobriety – Moon in Leo, in the 12th house.
- Full-time father to my five beautiful children – Jupiter in Capricorn, in 5th house.
- I have no personal social media accounts to request you follow me on – Saturn conjunct Ketu, in Scorpio, in the 3rd house.
- I am fully aware of the enemies my truth will create – Mars conjunct Venus, in the 6th house.
- Why would a sane man draft such a message – Sun conjunct Mercury, in Sagittarius, in the 4th house.
- I have been possessed by the Zeal of ANU – Jupiter trines Rahu, in the 9th house, at the same degree, in Taurus.

Do I not match the prophecies of the Puranas? Am I not from the West? Do I not preach veganism? Do I not preach sobriety? Who else knows, "The history of the future?" This *Golden Age* has long been forecasted. The stars speak a language that only the wise can interpret.

REVELATIONS UNSEALED: When a coincidence coincides

CHAPTER 7

CLARITY

Most preachers will not address the book of Revelations, yet alone reveal its true meaning. They cannot reveal because they do not understand. To understand this book, you must take it out of the biblical context and place it in a geographical context. Revelations is a book that covers the whole bible in its entirety from beginning to end.

The bible's history that King James authorized is only six thousand years old. That is nothing! Six thousand years is merely a drop in the bucket compared to how long man has been walking this earth. Right now they are finding artifacts millions of years old, which supports my stance, that we must look to the earth for the answers.

RH negative bloodlines has ruled this world for an exceedingly long time and rightfully so; they are generally smarter and healthier. RH negative bloodlines are immune to many diseases because their body contain antibodies, which cause some to believe, that these elites (RH negatives) are creating diseases to wipeout the masses (RH positives). The overwhelming majority of RH negative bloodlines resides in Europe, better known as *The Dragon's Crown*. Corona is Latin for 'crown'.

Not all RH negatives are malicious, some are benevolent, my mother being an example. But make no mistake, the people in positions of power across the globe are of RH negative decent. The Georgia Guide Stone's population represent a world without RH positives; this is their goal! The *psalter map* shows us how they plan on surviving the apocalypse; but ANU's wrath shall not be avoided.

Let us no longer be separated by language and culture. Weather using the term 'Anunnaki's return', 'Chandler's wobble', or simply referring to *Isaiah 14:16*, the same energy that has visited earth before is coming again. Regardless of your blood type choose righteousness; judgement day is nearby. This world is going burn out and ANU will create a new world only with the righteous.

REPENT SERPENT.

REVELATIONS UNSEALED: When a coincidence coincides

Be wise as the serpent! We must not rely on them to spread our message!

SCAN ME

REVELATIONS UNSEALED: When a coincidence coincides

Made in the USA
Coppell, TX
23 February 2022

74030822R00029